CHECKERBOARD BIOGRAPHIES

# MUHAMMAD ALI

JESSICA RUSICK

Checkerboard
Library

An Imprint of Abdo Publishing
abdobooks.com

# ABDOBOOKS.COM

Published by Abdo Publishing, a division of ABDO, PO Box 398166, Minneapolis, Minnesota 55439. Copyright © 2022 by Abdo Consulting Group, Inc. International copyrights reserved in all countries. No part of this book may be reproduced in any form without written permission from the publisher. Checkerboard Library™ is a trademark and logo of Abdo Publishing.

Printed in the United States of America, North Mankato, Minnesota
052021
092021

Design and Production: Mighty Media, Inc.
Editor: Liz Salzmann
Cover Photograph: The Stanley Weston Archive/Getty Images
Interior Photographs: AP Images, pp. 13, 15, 17, 19, 21, 28 (top, bottom right), 29 (top left, bottom left); Carol M. Highsmith/Library of Congress, pp. 27, 29 (bottom right); Paul Morse/National Archives and Records Administration, pp. 25, 29; Ralph Dominguez/MediaPunch/MediaPunch/IPx/AP Images, p. 5; Shutterstock Images, pp. 11 (paper clip), 11, 23; The Courier-Journal/Wikimedia Commons, p. 7; Wikimedia Commons, pp. 9, 28

Library of Congress Control Number: 2021932876

**Publisher's Cataloging-in-Publication Data**
Names: Rusick, Jessica, author.
Title: Muhammad Ali / by Jessica Rusick
Description: Minneapolis, Minnesota : Abdo Publishing, 2022 | Series: Checkerboard biographies | Includes online resources and index.
Identifiers: ISBN 9781532195969 (lib. bdg.) | ISBN 9781098216825 (ebook)
Subjects: LCSH: Ali, Muhammad, 1942-2016 (Cassius Marcellus Clay Jr.)--Juvenile literature. | African American boxers--Biography--Juvenile literature. | Boxers (Sports)--United States--Biography--Juvenile literature. | Philanthropists--Biography--Juvenile literature. | Civil rights workers--Biography--Juvenile literature. | Professional athletes--United States--Biography--Juvenile literature.
Classification: DDC 796.83092--dc23

# CONTENTS

| | |
|---|---|
| THE GREATEST | 4 |
| A BORN BOXER | 6 |
| RISING STAR | 8 |
| HEAVYWEIGHT CHAMP | 10 |
| SUCCESS AND SETBACKS | 12 |
| BACK TO BOXING | 16 |
| TWO-TIME CHAMPION | 18 |
| SIGNS OF DECLINE | 20 |
| RETIREMENT | 22 |
| CHARITABLE CHAMP | 24 |
| FOREVER GREAT | 26 |
| TIMELINE | 28 |
| GLOSSARY | 30 |
| ONLINE RESOURCES | 31 |
| INDEX | 32 |

## CHAPTER 1

# THE GREATEST

**Muhammad Ali was a boxer and activist.** He is known as one of the greatest boxers and athletes of all time. Ali was also an admired public figure.

Ali was born Cassius Marcellus Clay Jr. He began boxing at a young age. Ali soon became known for his unique fighting style. He was also known for his quick wit and charm.

Ali won his first heavyweight championship in 1964. He went undefeated for years, earning the nickname "The Greatest." At the height of his career, Ali was banned from professional boxing for refusing to fight in the **Vietnam War**. But Ali did not let this setback stop him. He remained outspoken even when his beliefs were unpopular. When Ali returned to boxing, he claimed the heavyweight title twice more.

After retiring from boxing, Ali was **diagnosed** with Parkinson's disease. But Ali continued to make a difference. He raised millions of dollars for Parkinson's research and other causes. Ali died in 2016. But he would forever be remembered as The Greatest.

Ali once said he wanted to be remembered as a man who treated everyone right.

## CHAPTER 2

# A BORN BOXER

**Cassius Marcellus Clay Jr. was born on January 17, 1942, in Louisville, Kentucky.** His father, Cassius Marcellus Sr., painted signs and murals. His mother, Odessa Grady, worked as a cook and maid. Cassius had a younger brother named Rudolph.

During Cassius's childhood, the South was racially **segregated**. Many restaurants, parks, schools, and other public places were for "whites only." Later in life, Cassius would speak out against racial **discrimination**.

When Cassius was 12, his bike was stolen. He reported the theft to a police officer named Joe Martin. Cassius was angry. He told Martin he wanted to fight the thief. Martin replied that Cassius had first better learn to fight.

In his spare time, Martin ran a gym and trained young boxers. He suggested Cassius join the gym and try boxing. Cassius was eager to try the new sport. When he visited the gym, he was excited by the sights, sounds, and smells of the boxing ring.

Cassius soon began training with Martin. Martin was impressed by Cassius's drive and talent. Just six weeks into training, Martin selected Cassius to appear on a locally televised fight. Cassius won!

**Cassius with Martin (*right*). Martin was an early supporter of civil rights in Louisville. Unlike many other public places, his gym was not segregated.**

## CHAPTER 3

# RISING STAR

**Over the next years, Clay continued to train with Martin.** From 1956 to 1959, he won several national amateur boxing titles. Clay was hard to beat. In 100 fights, he lost just 8 times.

In 1960, Clay graduated from Louisville's Central High School. Later that year, he was chosen for the US Olympic team as a light-heavyweight boxer. Clay traveled to Rome, Italy, for the Olympics. There, he beat Polish boxer Zbigniew Pietrzykowski to win the gold medal.

### FEAR OF FLYING

Clay was terrified of flying. This fear almost stopped him from going to the Olympics. Eventually, Martin convinced Clay to go. But Clay brought a **parachute** on the plane in case it crashed!

Clay's medal made him a star when he returned to Louisville. He soon caught the attention of a group of local business leaders. They were called the Louisville Sponsoring Group. The group paid for Clay's training and helped him turn professional.

Clay quickly moved up the professional heavyweight boxing ranks. He won his first 19 professional fights,

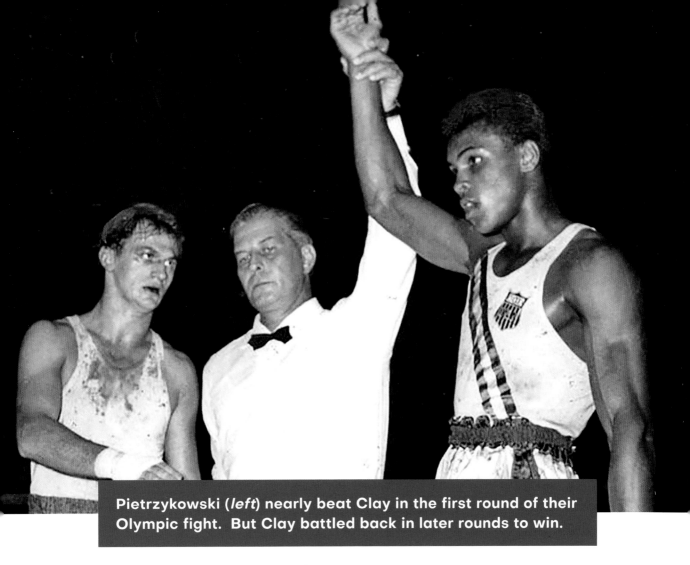

Pietrzykowski (*left*) nearly beat Clay in the first round of their Olympic fight. But Clay battled back in later rounds to win.

including 15 knockouts. In 1963, he appeared on the cover of *Time* magazine. Clay's rising star soon earned him the biggest fight of his career. He would fight Sonny Liston, the heavyweight champion of the world, for his title.

## CHAPTER 4

# HEAVYWEIGHT CHAMP

**Most sports writers believed Clay was no match for Liston.** They viewed Clay as too inexperienced. Many boxing experts also disliked Clay's unusual boxing style.

Clay saw himself as a showman. He joked and bragged to reporters before matches. He taunted his opponents with short, funny poems. Clay was called "The Louisville Lip" for his **confident**, talkative nature.

On February 25, 1964, Clay and Liston fought for the heavyweight title. Clay's fighting style worked to his advantage. He was fast and light on his feet, throwing punches with precision. Liston could not keep up.

After six rounds, Liston was too battered to continue. Clay was the new heavyweight champion of the world! At 22 years old, he was also the youngest in history. Many people were shocked by Clay's victory.

But Clay was not surprised. He showed his usual confidence, shouting "I am the greatest!" Clay would be known as "The Greatest" for much of his career.

# BIO BASICS

**NAMES:** Cassius Marcellus Clay Jr.; Muhammad Ali

**NICKNAMES:** The Louisville Lip, The Greatest

**BIRTH:** January 17, 1942, Louisville, Kentucky

**DEATH:** June 3, 2016

**SPOUSES:** Sonji Roi (1964-1966); Belinda Boyd (1967-1977); Veronica Porche (1977-1986); Yolanda "Lonnie" Williams (1986-2016)

**CHILDREN:** Jamillah, Rasheda, Maryum, Muhammad Ali Jr., Miya, Khaliah, Hana, Laila, Asaad

**FAMOUS FOR:** being one of the best boxers of all time and a respected public figure

**ACHIEVEMENTS:** winning the heavyweight title three times; in the International Boxing Hall of Fame; receiving the Presidential Medal of Freedom

**CHAPTER 5**

# SUCCESS AND SETBACKS

**Days after his victory against Liston, Clay once again surprised the world.** He announced that he had converted to **Islam**. On March 6, 1964, Clay changed his name to Muhammad Ali.

In August 1964, Ali married Sonji Roi. The marriage ended in 1966. Meanwhile, Ali defended his heavyweight title. On May 25, 1965, he faced Liston in a rematch. Ali knocked out Liston in the first round.

Ali defended his title several more times with commanding victories. In November 1966, Ali hit boxer Cleveland Williams 100 times in three rounds and earned a knockout. Williams landed just three punches on Ali during the match.

In 1967, Ali married Belinda Boyd. The couple went on to have four children. They are Jamillah, Rasheda,

 **I had the nerve to challenge the system, and all the people who hate injustice backed me for that.**

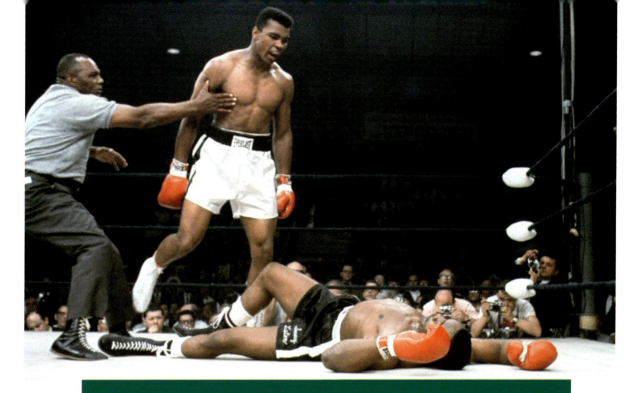

**In their rematch, Ali (*standing*) knocked out Liston in less than two minutes.**

Maryum, and Muhammad Ali Jr. Ali also had two children outside of the marriage, Miya and Khaliah.

Ali soon faced one of the most trying times in his career. Since 1964, the United States had been at war in Vietnam. Many American men were **drafted** to fight. Ali was drafted in 1967. But he felt fighting in the war went against his religious beliefs. So, Ali refused to join the US military.

Ali faced harsh consequences for his actions. He was stripped of his heavyweight title and banned from professional boxing. This ban would last for three and a half years.

In June 1967, Ali was found guilty of **draft evasion**. He was sentenced to five years in prison. However, Ali remained out of prison on bail. His conviction was later overturned by the US **Supreme Court** in 1971.

At the time of Ali's ban, many Americans supported the **Vietnam War**. Ali was heavily criticized for his antiwar statements. But Ali stayed true to his beliefs. During his ban from boxing, he gave lectures at colleges across the country. At the lectures, Ali spoke out against the war. He also spoke in support of the **civil rights** movement.

Over the next years, the war in Vietnam became unpopular with Americans. So, public support for Ali began to increase again. Standing up for what he believed made Ali a respected public figure.

## BROADWAY BOXER

While he was banned from boxing, Ali starred in a Broadway musical called *Buck White*. Ali earned positive reviews. However, the musical closed soon after opening.

Ali's refusal to join the military was supported by civil rights leaders such as Martin Luther King Jr. (*third from right*).

## CHAPTER 6

# BACK TO BOXING

**Ali was allowed to return to boxing in 1970.** His first fight was against Jerry Quarry on October 26. Ali had lost some of his speed and strength during his time away from boxing. Still, he beat Quarry in three rounds.

During Ali's absence, Joe Frazier had become heavyweight champion. Now, Ali wanted his title back. On March 8, 1971, Ali battled Frazier in a match called the "Fight of the Century." It was the first time two undefeated heavyweight champions had faced each other.

The fight occurred at Madison Square Garden in New York City. Sports writers noted that Ali was not as light on his feet as he once was. For most of the fight, he did not move around the ring. Ali was also knocked down once by Frazier.

After 15 rounds, neither fighter had been knocked out. So, the match was decided by a group of judges. They declared Frazier the winner. It was the first loss of Ali's professional career.

Ali (*right*) was knocked down only four times in his career. He was never knocked unconscious.

## CHAPTER 7

# TWO-TIME CHAMPION

**Ali did not stay down for long.** Following his loss to Frazier, he won his next ten fights. And, he trained hard for a rematch with Frazier. In January 1974, Ali beat Frazier in a 12-round judge's decision.

Frazier had lost the heavyweight title to George Foreman in 1973. Ali's win against Frazier meant that he would face Foreman for the heavyweight title. The two fought on October 30, 1974. Their fight took place in the African country Zaire, which is now called the Democratic Republic of the Congo.

Many sports fans believed the aging Ali was no match for Foreman. But once again, Ali proved his doubters wrong. He used a new boxing method he called the "rope-a-dope." Instead of moving quickly around the ring, Ali leaned back against the ropes. This allowed him to easily avoid many of Foreman's punches.

By the end of the seventh round, Foreman had tired himself out. Ali then went on the offensive. He knocked Foreman out in the eighth round. Ali was once again the heavyweight champion!

Ali's (*right*) fight against Foreman was called the "Rumble in the Jungle" because of Zaire's large rain forests.

# CHAPTER 8
# SIGNS OF DECLINE

**On October 1, 1975, Ali's longtime rival Frazier once again challenged Ali for the heavyweight title.** Frazier's trainer stopped the fight after 14 rounds. Ali had successfully defended his title. But the match had been tough on both fighters. Ali said it had felt like he was dying.

In 1977, Ali and Belinda divorced. The same year, he married Veronica Porche. They had two daughters, Hana and Laila. Meanwhile, Ali's career began to decline. In 1978, he lost the heavyweight title to Leon Spinks.

## LIKE FATHER, LIKE DAUGHTER

Ali's daughter Laila also became a professional boxer. She won 24 fights and was undefeated in her eight-year career. Laila retired in 2007.

Ali earned the title back from Spinks later that year, becoming the first boxer ever to win the heavyweight title three times. But those close to Ali worried fighting was taking a physical toll on him. His **reflexes** were slower. And, sometimes he was unable to speak clearly. These are signs of illness. Ali's doctors, friends, and family members urged him to retire.

Ali (*left*) assumed he would win his first fight with Spinks. So, he did not spend much time training. Ali devoted more time to training for the rematch.

## CHAPTER 9

# RETIREMENT

**Ali retired from boxing in 1979.** However, he returned the next year to fight once more for the heavyweight title. Ali lost in an 11-round match to champion Larry Holmes.

In 1981, Ali also lost to Jamaican boxer Trevor Berbick by judge's decision. After the fight, Ali acknowledged he was no longer in his prime. "Nothing lasts forever, not even Muhammad Ali," he said. The Berbick fight was the last of Ali's career. He retired from boxing for good in 1981. He had a career record of 56 wins, 5 losses, and 37 knockouts.

In 1984, Ali was **diagnosed** with Parkinson's disease. This nervous system condition affects movement and speech. The disease is usually **genetic**. But some doctors believe head **trauma** during Ali's boxing career could have contributed to it. There is no cure for Parkinson's. But Ali took medicine to ease his **symptoms**.

In 1986, Ali and Veronica divorced. He married Yolanda "Lonnie" Williams later that year. The couple adopted a son, Asaad.

Ali stops outside an airport to sign autographs in 1979. Throughout his life, Ali loved to meet and entertain fans.

## CHAPTER 10
# CHARITABLE CHAMP

**Ali earned many honors after his retirement.** In 1990, he was entered into the International Boxing Hall of Fame. In 1996, Ali was chosen to light the flame to start the Olympic Games in Atlanta, Georgia.

In 1997, Ali helped found the Muhammad Ali Parkinson Center in Arizona. The center works to treat, research, and educate the public about Parkinson's. Ali partnered with a charity called Celebrity Fight Night to raise money for the center. Through his work, Ali raised an estimated $100 million to fight Parkinson's.

Ali championed several other causes. He worked with organizations such as Make-A-Wish and the Special Olympics. In 2005, Ali helped found the Muhammad Ali Center. This museum promotes respect and understanding in the world. The same year, Ali was awarded the Presidential Medal of Freedom.

> *I've always wanted to be more than just a boxer ... I wanted to use my fame, and this face that everyone knows so well, to help uplift and inspire people around the world.*

President George W. Bush (*right*) awarded the Presidential Medal of Freedom to Ali on November 9, 2005. He called Ali "a fierce fighter and man of peace."

### CHAPTER 11

# FOREVER GREAT

**Over the next years, Parkinson's made it increasingly difficult for Ali to move and communicate.** So, he rarely gave public interviews. Ali instead liked to spend time with family at his home in Arizona. He enjoyed watching old movies and TV shows.

Ali was admitted to the hospital several times in the 2010s. On May 30, 2016, he was treated for a breathing problem. Family and friends believed he would battle back like before. But Ali's condition worsened. He died on June 3, 2016. He was 74 years old.

People from all around the world paid tribute to Ali's remarkable life. Thousands gathered for a memorial service in Louisville. Sports stars, presidents, **civil rights** leaders, and more remembered Ali as an icon. Ali would forever be known for his athleticism, charm, and generosity.

" He who is not courageous enough to take risks will accomplish nothing in life. "

Ali is buried at Cave Hill Cemetery in Louisville.

# TIMELINE

**1942**
Cassius Marcellus Clay Jr. is born on January 17 in Louisville, Kentucky.

**1964**
Clay defeats Sonny Liston to earn the heavyweight title. Clay converts to Islam and changes his name to Muhammad Ali.

**1970**
Ali returns to boxing following his ban.

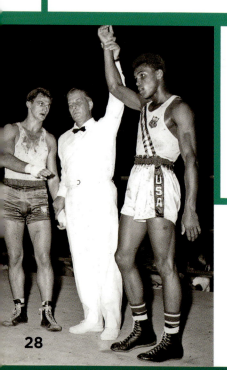

**1960**
Clay wins a gold medal for boxing at the Olympic Games in Rome, Italy.

**1967**
Ali refuses to fight in the Vietnam War for religious reasons. For this, he is stripped of his heavyweight title and banned from professional boxing.

### 1978
Ali loses the heavyweight title to Leon Spinks. Ali reclaims it later that year, becoming the first boxer to become heavyweight champion three times.

### 1984
Ali is diagnosed with Parkinson's disease.

### 2005
Ali receives the Presidential Medal of Freedom.

### 1974
Ali wins the heavyweight title from George Foreman.

### 1981
Ali retires from boxing.

### 1997
Ali helps found the Muhammad Ali Parkinson Center.

### 2016
Muhammad Ali dies on June 3 at the age of 74.

# GLOSSARY

**activist**—a person who takes direct action in support of or in opposition to an issue that causes disagreement.

**civil rights**—rights that protect people from unequal treatment or discrimination.

**confident**—having faith in your own abilities. This feeling is confidence.

**diagnose**—to recognize something, such as a disease, by signs, symptoms, or tests.

**discrimination** (dihs-krih-muh-NAY-shuhn)—unfair treatment, often based on race, religion, or gender.

**draft**—a system for or act of selecting individuals from a group. People may be drafted for required military service or sports teams.

**evasion**—the act of escaping or avoiding something.

**genetic**—relating to or involving genes.

**Islam**—the religion of Muslims as described in the Koran. It is based on the teachings of the god Allah through the Prophet Muhammad.

**parachute**—an umbrella-like device consisting of fabric from which a person or object is suspended. A parachute is used to slow something falling through the air.

**reflexes**—a person's ability to react quickly.

**segregate**—to separate an individual or a group from a larger group, especially by race.

**Supreme Court**—the highest, most powerful court in the United States.

**symptom**—a noticeable change in the normal working of the body. A symptom indicates or accompanies disease, sickness, or other malfunction.

**trauma**—a wound or injury to the body or the mind.

**Vietnam War**—from 1954 to 1975. A long, failed attempt by the United States to stop North Vietnam from taking over South Vietnam.

# ONLINE RESOURCES

To learn more about Muhammad Ali, please visit **abdobooklinks.com** or scan this QR code. These links are routinely monitored and updated to provide the most current information available.

# INDEX

activism, 4, 6, 13, 14, 24
Africa, 18
awards and honors, 24

ban from boxing, 4, 14, 16
Berbick, Trevor, 22
birth, 4, 6
Boxing Hall of Fame, 24
boxing style, 4, 10, 18
boxing titles, 4, 8, 10, 12, 16, 18, 20

Celebrity Fight Night, 24
charitable work, 4, 24
childhood, 4, 6, 7, 8
civil rights, 14, 26
criminal charges, 14

death, 4, 26

education, 8

family, 6, 12, 13, 20, 22, 26
Foreman, George, 18
Frazier, Joe, 16, 18, 20

health, 4, 20, 22, 26
Holmes, Larry, 22

Islam, 12, 13
Italy, 8

Liston, Sonny, 9, 10, 12
Louisville Sponsoring Group, 8

Make-A-Wish, 24
Martin, Joe, 6, 7, 8
military draft, 13, 14
Muhammad Ali Parkinson Center, 24

nicknames, 4, 10

Olympic Games, 8, 24

Parkinson's disease, 4, 22, 24, 26
Pietrzykowski, Zbigniew, 8
Poland, 8
Presidential Medal of Freedom, 24

Quarry, Jerry, 16

retirement, 4, 20, 22, 24

segregation, 6
Special Olympics, 24
Spinks, Leon, 20
Supreme Court, US, 14

*Time* magazine, 9
training, 6, 7, 8, 18

United States, 6, 8, 13, 14, 16, 24, 26

Vietnam War, 4, 13, 14

Williams, Cleveland, 12